In Reality: Selected Poems

T0162958

SEREN DISCOVERIES

Other translations from Seren Discoveries include

In Reality: Selected Poems
Jean Portante

Translated by Zoë Skoulding

Seren is the book imprint of
Poetry Wales Press Ltd
Nolton Street, Bridgend, Wales

www.serenbooks.com
facebook.com/SerenBooks
Twitter: @SerenBooks

Original French text © Jean Portante
Translation © Zoë Skoulding, 2013

This translation is published with the support of Le Gouvernement du
Grand-Duché de Luxembourg: Ministère de la Culture.

LE GOUVERNEMENT
DU GRAND-DUCHÉ DE LUXEMBOURG
Ministère de la Culture

The right of Jean Portante to be identified
as the Author of this Work has been asserted
in accordance with the Copyright, Designs
and Patents Act, 1988.

ISBN 978-1-78172-065-3
Mobi: 978-1-78172-066-0
Epub: 978-1-78172-057-7

Cover art by Robert Brandy.

A CIP record for this title is available from
the British Library.

All rights reserved. No part of this publication
may be reproduced, stored in a retrieval system,
or transmitted at any time or by any means
electronic, mechanical, photocopying, recording
or otherwise without the prior permission
of the copyright holders.

The publisher works with the financial assistance
of the Welsh Books Council.

Printed by the Grosvenor Group (Print Services) Ltd, London

L'oubli détient le pouvoir et le sens du secret.

Maurice Blanchot

Table des Matières

Contents

Translator's Preface

What happens when language itself is subjected to the tremors of an earthquake? Jean Portante's sonnet sequence *Ce qui advient et ce qui n'advient pas,* or *What does and what doesn't come to pass* (Red Fox Press, 2010), asks this question with reference to the 2009 earthquake that destroyed San Demetrio. This Italian village close to L'Aquila was not Portante's birthplace but it resonates through his work as the home of his ancestors and a place where he spent part of his childhood. Most of the houses are still standing, their old stone construction appearing from the outside to be holding up. However, they are entirely unsafe; their inhabitants are forbidden to enter them and have been moved to temporary housing across the valley. Portante's poems, written not in his mother tongue, Italian, but in his adopted language, French, create a similarly broken architecture. They are full of lyric memory yet offer no return to a familiar origin, only an 'I' full of echoes. It's writing that never seems quite at home with itself, its nomadic, unsettled quality drawing attention to a French inflected by its coexistence with other languages.

Widely translated, Portante's prolific output has been recognised by numerous prizes and awards in France, Luxembourg, and across the world. The appeal of his work lies not only in its startling, off-kilter images and unusual musicality, but also in a relationship to language that is more common outside of monolingual Anglophone environments than it is within them. He was born to Italian immigrant parents in the steel mining town of Differdange, Luxembourg, and he grew up speaking Italian alongside Luxembourgish, German and French, the language in which he ultimately chose to write. He later lived through Spanish for several years while working in Cuba, and has translated numerous poets from all the above languages as well as English. The fact that his work does not fit comfortably into a single national tradition – that it is already inhabited by forms of transition and translation – makes it on the one hand expressive of a very personal set of cultural co-ordinates, and on the other, wholly European, holding within itself the contradictions and complexities of plural languages. Then again, Luxembourg itself is multilingual and full of migrants from Italy, Portugal and elsewhere, not to mention those who travel to work across its borders each day from Germany and France, so perhaps this rubbing against the grain of national identity is, paradoxically, quintessentially Luxembourgish.

The task of the translator, as explained in Walter Benjamin's well-known essay, is to make one's own language foreign, and one of the excitements of translating this work has been to see what it does to English, a language so globally dominant that it needs to be inhabited in as many ways as possible to counter-act its homogenising tendencies. Coming across Portante's poetry for the first time, I was struck by its contrasts: jolts and swerves of syntax disupt its powerful lyric fluency, while every-day objects are juxtaposed with matter-of-fact mythological reference. Images are compressed and multiplied to the point of instability. Nouns take on a life of their own, particularly when used without articles, which in French edges them towards personification, the gendered pronouns intensifying the impression of a world in which things are expressively alive, while the 'I' of the poems remains elusive and multiple. Such poetry would probably not be written in English, and its translation cannot be easily absorbed into any of the more obvious modes of contemporary UK poetry. Nevertheless, translating with too direct an echo of French could create an over-formal register because French comes to English with a freight of associations from a cultural past dominated by French and Latin-speaking elites, whereas Portante's work emerges from the struggles of an industrial working class, his affiliations with Latin America inflecting a vision of poetry as language's revolutionary freedom. If the task of the poet, as Portante himself has often stressed, is not to write in any given language but in his or her own language (*malangue*), the situa-tion of the poet between languages, who inhabits a language from a marginal or outsider's position, enriches the possibili-ties for doing this. Translation begins within the poems themselves, and the translation into English has been another step in this continuing process.

The selection offered here from four recent collections, presented in reverse chronological order, covers a relatively short time span yet includes themes that have long been important in Portante's work. *What does and what doesn't come to pass*, published by Red Fox in 2010 as an artist's book by Robert Brandy (from which the cover image of this book is taken), raises persistently a question that is central to migrant experience: how does place survive in the memory of a lost community? This question is as relevant to those who have lost their homes in the L'Aquila earthquake as it is to the families who left Italy for Luxembourg in search of work throughout the first half of the twentieth century. The slowness of the restoration project in the L'Aquila region is a matter of pressing concern because the longer it takes, the slighter the hope is of communities being restored along with the buildings. When social space is ruptured, it is harder to mend than bricks and mortar because it depends on a rich mesh of habit and memory; its loss is a shared cultural loss.

What Portante doesn't do is try to hold on to memory of place through any kind of realist documentation. As soon as memory is put into words, it becomes fiction, and this dialogue between memory and forgetting is explored in *La réinvention de l'oubli* or *The Reinvention of Forgetting* (Le Castor Astral, 2010). Only in forgetting can memory remain intact; once articulated, everything is subject to distortion. Poetry becomes a means of navigating the unspoken, but these poems also heighten and foreground the mythologies that reverberate in language. The looking back of Orpheus is never far away, yet classical references are interwoven with more personal and idiosyncratic imagery.

Translating this work meant negotiating a distinctive blend of the metaphysical and the mundane that inhabits French more easily, perhaps, than English. The word *oubli* itself is a case in point: the available choices in English are 'forgetting' or 'oblivion', which have differing degrees of abstraction and formality, whereas in French the forgetting of one's keys or the deep forgetfulness of the self in oblivion are both expressed by the same word. I have favoured 'forgetting' to keep a more concrete sense, though either would be possible. Elsewhere the problem was different: *mémoire*, the faculty of memory, and *souvenir*, a specific memory, collapse into each other in English as they don't in French.

The overall title of this selection, *In Reality*, is taken from the collection *En réalité* (Phi, 2008). Hovering between a location in 'the real' and a turn of phrase, it's a title that encapsulates the tension between world and word in Portante's writing. Here, an invented mythology is drawn from the planets and from physical elements. Before modern techniques of steelmaking concealed the process, the gush of red molten iron ore was part of the industrial landscape of Differdange; the imagery of the inferno was ever-present and red dust settled on every surface. However, where the poems seem to evoke the physical world, for example in the image of red earth crushed in the hand, they do so within the limits of a mutable landscape where the red also becomes a 'ritual incandescence that makes and unmakes the horizon.' They present a challenge to 'be the accountant of one's own mythology' because we are all migrants in language, all of us creating our own provisional histories. The repetition in these poems of 'Je veux dire', which is translated in its ordinary sense as 'I mean', is literally in French 'I want to say', which insists more strongly on the space for what is unsaid between words and their multiplying fictions.

Finally, *Le travail du poumon*, or *The Work of the Lung* (Le Castor Astral, 2007), the earliest of the collections represented here, is the one that puts the most intense pressure on words themselves, which break down in parts of 'The Shadow Swimmer' into personal alphabetic codes. These moments elude translation: the play in IV between *cerf* (stag), *mort* (death) and *nord* (north) works on a continuity of sound in the words that links personal experience with the geographies of migration; likewise in VIII the 'furious consonant' that differentiates *mort* from *mot* (word) remains stubbornly located in French despite the poem's insistence on the capacity of language to 'err'.

The migratory sensibility of this writing is also expressed in the image of the whale, the metaphor explored in Portante's novel *Mrs Haroy ou la memoire de la baleine* (Phi, 1993) and echoed in his poetry. The whale's evolution is a history of migration from land to sea, with its redundant lung creating a certain awkwardness in its element that comes from a hidden memory of a different existence. As Portante writes:

> [...] there isn't ONE language in my writing. What you see is the French language, a little disordered but on the whole correct, I mean orthographically, morphologically and syntactically speaking. What isn't seen, what only exists inside, 'lungs' [*poumonne*] the plurality of languages, the mother tongue and others, without revealing itself.

(*Poetry Wales* 46.3, 2011, p. 10)

His French is inflected by breathing from elsewhere, sometimes compressed and contorted, sometimes echoing Italian in its rhythmical and syntactical emphasis on the beginning of a phrase rather than its end. There are also trans-lingual puns, as Portante notes:

> ... when I write *bougie* and so evoke light, on the inside the Italian word *bugia*, which means 'lie', is 'lunging' and attracting around it a darker semantic field[...]; it is necessary to erase the language one sees in order to read the plurality of languages.

(*Poetry Wales* 46.3, 2011, p. 11)

Such subtleties clearly cannot survive English translation, but they are just as lost in translation to Italian. Portante's *effaçonnements* (his neologism suggesting 'erasings-creations') are central to the process of translation itself, which erases the source language as well as re-creating the new text. What does carry through these encounters is breath – the breath of a line, where breathing itself is heard and felt as a conscious action that travels across languages and joins them together, multiplying the ways in language and therefore the world may be inhabited.

CE QUI ADVIENT ET CE QUI N'ADVIENT PAS

WHAT DOES AND WHAT DOESN'T COME TO PASS

2010

Je suis devenue immatérielle,
ombre qui se déplace dans la flamme
de la mort perpétuelle.
Mario Luzi

De ce qui advient ou n'advient pas l'ombre est me semble-t-il le fantôme le moins expérimenté. Non que de l'un à l'autre le double témoin comme qui aurait décidé de tendre une oreille ou de figer son souffle se souvienne de ce qui s'est passé. Je ne suis pas sûr que quelque chose se soit passé quand est remontée malgré l'obstruction des nuages une neige peu encline aux ascensions. Remontée vers où pourrait-on demander.

Ou que fait une neige quand au lieu de descendre elle monte. Ou pourquoi de ce qui advient ou n'advient pas ne jaillirait pas un autre fantôme qui là-bas s'est glissé dans l'hiver et ici dans les mots. Et pourquoi ce fantôme se glisserait-il dans les mots ici.

Of what does or doesn't come to pass the shadow is
it seems to me the least experienced ghost. Not
that between the two the double witness like someone
who'd decided to incline one ear or freeze his
breath would remember what had happened. I'm not
sure that that anything did happen when snow
not usually given to ascent rose again despite
the obstacle of clouds. Rose again to where
one might ask.
            Or what's snow doing
when instead of falling it rises. Or why
wouldn't another ghost well up from what
does or doesn't come to pass and slide down
there into winter and here into words. And why
would this ghost here slide into words.

Dans la poussière de ce qui a été quand s'y colle
non la farine mais une épaisseur des jours que ni
la pluie ni l'ombre ne savent déchiffrer – dans cette
poussière-là il survit à deux pas de lui-même le village
que surplombe la montagne. Loin trop loin de lui au
centre d'une cuisine où depuis longtemps le blé a été
remplacé par l'acier et l'acier par le souvenir le repas
qu'on prépare est le seul remède contre la perte de
l'oubli.

    Il y a une fissure invisible dans le flanc de la
montagne. Sur la colline d'en face la ruine et le château
lointain en connaissent l'histoire. Elles sont aussi
au-dessus dans le ciel la ruine et la fissure. Et il y en a
même dans le flanc de ta peau. On dirait un lac cicatrisé.
On dirait que rien n'a été recousu après l'opération.

In the dust of what's been when what sticks is
not flour but a thickness of days that neither
rain nor shadow knows how to decipher – in this
dust it survives at two steps from itself the village
that the mountain overhangs. Far much too far away
at the centre of a kitchen where wheat has long since been
replaced by steel and steel by memory the meal
prepared is the only cure for the loss of
forgetting.
       There's an unseen crack in the side of the
mountain. On the hill opposite the ruin and the distant
castle know the story. They're also up there in the sky
the ruin and the crack. And there even in the side
of your skin. You could say a scarred lake. You could say
nothing had been sewn up after the operation.

L'ombre non celle que le vent qui souffle dans la
braise peint sur le mur ni l'autre vue le long des
maisons ou à l'intérieur – l'ombre dis-je s'éloigne
de plus en plus de l'idée que je me fais d'une
ombre. Et même sans elle et sans toutes les autres
ombres qu'elles soient vivantes ou mortes l'idée que
je me fais s'éloigne.
                         Et elle s'éloigne également
du vent l'idée et de la braise sans parler du mur ou
des maisons. À tel point que je me demande à quoi
peut bien servir l'idée que je me fais des choses.
Qu'espères-tu lui dis-je. Que veux-tu vraiment.
Comme si la question était à elle seule la braise
qui fait danser les ombres. Ou le vent qui quand
il ne peint pas baisse les bras et rallume le mystère.

The shadow not the one that wind blowing in the embers
paints on the wall nor the other you can see along the
houses or inside – the shadow I say shifts
further and further from my idea of
shadow. And even without it and without all the other
shadows whether living or dead the idea I have
shifts.
      And the idea also shifts from the
wind and from the embers not to speak of the wall or
the houses. So much so that I wonder whether
the idea I have of things is any use at all.
What are you hoping for I ask it. What is it that you
really want. As if the question was only for the embers
that make the shadows dance. Or the wind that when
it isn't painting gives up and rekindles the mystery.

Surpris par le jour qui ne se lève plus la lune et
le soleil comme deux vieux voleurs souterrains
ont rallumé la torche et se sont mis en route. Je
suis sûr que qui de loin les aurait observés dans
leur pauvre lueur aurait eu pitié d'eux.

                                                      Ce qui
est sûr dans tout cela c'est que la nuit est tombée.
Et qu'une nuit qui tombe est quelque chose qui
hurle. Et que quand quelque chose hurle les voleurs
souterrains se servent de la torche. La torche
qui allume misérablement le ventre des choses
et fait éternuer les éléments. Ô hurlement des
éléments qui éternuent. Ô feu qui s'échappe du
ventre des choses. Et vous vieux voleurs savez-vous
maintenant à qui adresser vos excuses souterraines.

Surprised by day not breaking any more the moon
and the sun like two old underground thieves
relit the torch and set off. I'm sure that
anyone who'd seen their feeble glimmer from a
distance would have felt sorry for them.
                                        What is
certain here is that night fell. And that a night
falling is a howling thing. And that when
something howls the underground thieves
take the torch. The torch that weakly
lights the underside of things and makes the elements
sneeze. O howling of elements that sneeze.
O fire that escapes from the underside of things. And you
old thieves do you know now to whom you can
address your underground apologies.

Presque une image cette obscure attraction qui
fait couler les choses vers ce qui fuit l'éternel.
Combien de sommeil faut-il avant que ne soit
effacée la succession des nuits. Et combien en
faudra-t-il pour remettre de l'ordre dans la loi
des innocences.

Car dormir vois-tu est la galerie
innocente du temps. Et c'est à coups de pioches
et de pelles que se creuse la descente. Le soir
quand on s'y glisse cela fait longtemps que la nuit
attend les mains travailleuses. L'obscurité montre
le chemin. C'est elle le tunnel. C'est dans elle
que coulent les choses. Inutile de parler de
continuité. Ce qui fuit l'éternel quand résonnent
les coups des outils ne se fabrique ni ne dort jamais.

Nearly an image this dark attraction that makes things
stream towards what escapes the eternal.
How much sleep does it take before the succession
of nights is erased. And how much
does it take to bring back order to the law
of innocences.
                    Because sleep you see is the innocent
tunnel of time. And it's in blows of picks and
spades that descent is dug out. When you slide
down in the evening it's a long time that
night's been waiting for working hands. Darkness
shows the way. This is the tunnel. It's through
this that things stream. Useless to speak of continuity.
When the blows of tools ring out what escapes
the eternal neither manufactures itself nor ever sleeps.

Devant la grille fermée du cimetière comment ne pas me dire qu'il y a au moins une justice quand la terre est retournée. Ceux qui vivent resteront dehors cette fois. Et à l'intérieur – ce qui est mort. Visible enfin la frontière séparant les uns des autres. Une telle exclusion donne cependant presque envie de mourir.

On offrirait sa mort pour franchir le seuil. On désirerait furieusement qu'un passeur légendaire nous escorte jusqu'à l'autre côté pour voir ce qui s'y oublie. Tu m'entends j'en suis sûr l'appeler. Mais la grille ne s'ouvre pas. Est-il révolu le temps où pour un oui ou un non on entrait dans le pays de la mort. Est-ce dire que le retour est désormais impossible. Est-ce dire dis-moi que jamais plus tu ne reviendras.

In front of the closed gate of the cemetery how not
to say to myself that there's at least one justice
when the earth is turned over. Those who live will stay
outside this time. And inside – the dead.
Visible at last the frontier separating one from the other.
Such an exclusion however nearly makes you want
to die.
         We'd offer our deaths to cross the threshold.
We'd fiercely wish that a mythical ferryman
would take us to the other side to show us what's
forgotten there. I'm sure you hear me call him. But the
gate won't open. Has the time passed when you
could enter the land of the dead just like that.
Does this mean that return is impossible from now on.
Does this mean tell me that you'll never come back.

En avril parfois la terre comme si elle avait oublié
ses racines ferme les yeux et se remet en route.
Où va-t-elle personne ne le sait. On ne voit même
pas qu'elle se déplace. Et pourtant l'ébranlement
qui précède le voyage ne peut pas passer inaperçu.
Des rivières débordent des lacs se dessèchent des
églises sont englouties.

                                   Elle tremble la terre avant
de partir. Elle tremble de peur. C'est ainsi que
disparaît le noyau du temps. On dirait celui d'une
cerise morte recraché dans une cuvette vide. Mais
où va le noyau du temps quand la terre le recrache.
Va-t-il rebondir contre les cloches de l'église pour
donner le signal. Et où va la terre en avril. Quelle
route prend-elle la terre après avoir recraché le noyau.

Sometimes in April as if it had forgotten
its roots the earth shuts its eyes and sets off.
Where it's going no-one knows. You don't even
see it move. And yet the shuddering
before the journey cannot pass unnoticed.
Rivers overflow lakes dry up churches
are swallowed.
                    It trembles the earth before
leaving. It trembles with fear. It's like this
that the core of time disappears. You could say
it's the stone of a dead cherry spat out in an empty basin. But
where does the core of time go when the earth spits it out.
Will it rebound against church clocks to give
the signal. And where does the earth go in April. What
road does it take having spat out the core.

La voici la limite du domaine avec ses introuvables
tristesses revenant comme une rivière sans lit vers
ses nuages. De là-haut un peu avant de s'endormir et
de penser à ce qu'on dira de ceux qui ainsi font défaut –
de là-haut l'étendue qu'elle embrasse est désormais un
vaste brouillard avec ses ouvriers et ses machines
malaxant l'ombre de l'air.

        Ceux qui là-bas creusent sont
les artisans d'un univers abandonné. Leurs mains imitent
les pelles du destin. Il leur faudrait un oiseau de blanc
augure pour venir à bout du travail. Une flèche ne
revenant pas du soleil mais d'un système qu'aucun
pas n'a encore foulé. Il leur faudrait une côte plus
escarpée que celle d'où retombe sans cesse la pierre.
Et une brume dessinant pour qui s'y perd les contours.

Here it is the boundary with its unfindable
sadnesses returning like a river with no bed towards
its clouds. From up there just before sleeping and
thinking of what to say to those who are missing –
from up there the stretch it embraces will now be a
vast fog with its workers and machines
kneading the air's shadow.
                          Those digging over there are
the architects of an abandoned universe. Their hands are
mimicking the spades of destiny. They'd need a bird of white
augury to finish their work. An arrow not
returning from the sun but from a system in which
no-one has yet set foot. They'd need a steeper slope
than the one from which the stone keeps rolling back.
And a mist to draw the contours for those who are lost.

Quand par terre ne reste que l'ombre et dans le ciel
le soleil et pas de corps ni de maisons ni d'arbres à
perte de vue – quand tout ça la tristesse cosmique
n'a plus d'objet. Elle qui vivait du va-et-vient des
choses dit alors au temps et à ceux qui le gèrent
d'arrêter le décompte.

Arrêtez de compter dit-elle
ou comptez à voix basse. Ou allez compter ailleurs.
Là où le mystère est un fil et le corps une femme
et la maison une naissance. C'est là qu'il faut
recommencer à compter. C'est là qu'un arbre est
le premier arbre et un autre le deuxième et le temps
qui passe une somme confortable. Car qui vit dans
sa naissance n'a pas besoin d'ombre.

Et qui a le corps
d'une femme tient par un bout le fil du mystère.

When nothing stays on the ground but shadow and
in the sky the sun and no bodies nor houses nor trees as far as
the eye can see – when it comes to all this the cosmic sadness
loses its purpose. The sadness that lived in the coming and
going of things tells time and those who manage it
to stop counting.
                              Stop counting it says
or count quietly. Or go and count somewhere else.
There where strangeness is a thread and the body a woman
and the house a birth. It's there that you have to
start counting again. It's there that a tree is
the first tree and another the second and time
that passes an easy sum. Because whatever lives in its
birth doesn't need shadow.
                              And whoever has a woman's
body holds one end of the thread of strangeness.

Que t'a dit cette nuit-là alors que l'axe des choses
se déplaçait imperceptiblement vers le fracas – que
t'a dit la fumée qui de la cuisine se glissait par la
fenêtre entre-ouverte. Tu étais souviens-toi dos à dos
avec le mur d'en face. Quelqu'un t'avait demandé de
sortir. Et à présent la fumée sortait elle aussi et elle t'a
parlé la fumée et tu gardes le silence.

                            Tu es le gardien
du silence à présent. Et tu es dos à dos avec le mur.
Et vers le fracas se déplace imperceptiblement
l'axe des choses. Elle est grandiose cette nuit-là
mais elle n'a plus de mots. Et puisque la fumée
parle et ne te parle qu'à toi et que tu es le gardien
du silence qui me dira mon amour de combien
de brûlures cette fumée-là était la porte-parole.

What did that night say to you while the axis of things
shifted imperceptibly towards fracas – what did
the smoke say to you as it slid from the kitchen through
the half-open window. You had do you remember your
back against the opposite wall. Someone had asked you to
leave. And now the smoke it was leaving too and it
spoke to you the smoke and you keep silent.
                                              You are
the guardian of silence now. And your back is against
the wall. And towards fracas the axis of things
imperceptibly shifts. It is magnificent that night
but it has no more words. And because the smoke
speaks and speaks to you and only to you and as you are
the guardian of silence who will tell me my love
for how many burnings that smoke was the speaker.

Si au fond du lac l'église engloutie n'a pas
tremblé c'est parce que les légendes sont de vieux
coquillages aux murs solides. Ses cloches n'ont pas
sonné quand au-dessus le signal a été donné. Aucun
corps de nageur n'a été réclamé cet été.

Ceux qui
malgré tout se sont aventurés au-delà de la crevasse
ont su résister aux histoires qu'au coin d'aucun feu on
se raconte. L'eau se serait dit-on retirée en elle-même
comme une spirale sans bride vrillant vers sa
disparition. Mais que mouille encore une eau ainsi
engloutie sinon la revanche de mouiller. Que cherchait
jadis le corps du nageur quand août après août par le
sacrifice de sa noyade il réanimait les vieilles histoires
qu'on ne se raconte plus en aucun coin du feu.

If at the bottom of the lake the swallowed church
didn't tremble it's because the legends are old
shells with solid walls. Its bells made no
sound at the signal given above. No swimmer's
body was reclaimed that summer.
                                    Those who
despite everything ventured beyond the crack
knew how to resist the tales told by the side of
any fire. It's said the water would have been drawn
into itself an unbridled spiral drilling towards its
disappearance. But what can such swallowed water
still moisten if not the return of moisture. What was he
looking for long ago the swimmer when August after August
the sacrifice of his drowned body brought to life
the old tales that no-one tells now by the side of any fire.

Que reste-t-il de l'ombre quand rien n'est plus
à sa place. Lutte-t-elle contre elle-même comme
une mer inexpérimentée sur laquelle ne bouge aucun
navire. Où iront se briser les vagues au moment du
repos.

Ou est-elle comme un Icare l'ombre – tout près
d'un soleil prenant son élan non pour tomber mais pour
écrire la dernière page du bonheur que ne lui a promis
aucun destin. La voilà là-haut montant sans cesse
et ce qui tombe n'est que son ombre qui s'éloigne
et s'éloignant s'éloigne également de la mer – la mer
sur laquelle ne bouge aucun navire. Et rien n'est plus
à sa place. Et du bonheur promis quelques pétales
brûlent déjà. Et aucun Icare n'est plus en route. Il n'y
a qu'un migrateur là-haut luttant contre lui-même.

What's left of the shadow when nothing
is left in its place. Does it fight with itself like
an inexperienced sea on which no ship
moves. Where will the waves break at the moment
of coming to rest.
                         Or is it like an Icarus the shadow – up close
to a sun using its momentum not to fall but to
write the last page of happiness that no destiny
has promised it. Up there climbing endlessly
and what falls is only its shadow which leaves
and in leaving leaves the sea as well – the sea on which
no ship moves. And nothing is left in its place any more.
And from the promised happiness some petals are already
burning. And there's no Icarus on his way any more. There's
only a migrant up there fighting with himself.

From:

LA RÉINVENTION DE L'OUBLI

THE REINVENTION OF FORGETTING

2010

Prémices de l'oubli

Ma mère me dit où ai-je mis
LA LUNE
et elle pose la lune dans l'évier :

puis elle me dit la lune me glisse du cerveau
et elle roule je ne sais où à l'intérieur :

puis elle se tait si définitivement que je me dis
qu'elle a tout dit et que le silence ultime existe :

puis la lune dans l'évier se rappelle
à mon souvenir si définitivement
que je me dis qu'elle aussi a tout dit
et que le silence ultime existe.

Preludes to Forgetting

My mother says to me where did I put
THE MOON
and she puts the moon in the sink:

then she says the moon slips from my brain
and rolls around I don't know where inside:

then she stops talking so definitively I say to myself
she's said everything and ultimate silence exists:

then the moon in the sink comes
to mind so definitively
that I say to myself it too has said everything
and ultimate silence exists.

Toi au printemps
quand la nature est encore
SOUS LE CHOC DES NEIGES
qui ne tombent plus
toi quand tu refais le compte
des fentes dans le mur
ou que tu refais également
le compte des fentes dans ta peau
ou que tu égrènes comme un chapelet
d'étoiles arrachées à la prière de l'univers
les rides sur l'écorce terrestre
ou les pattes d'oie
qui te ferment les yeux :

toi quand tu refais tout
ça la montagne
– celle qui n'est plus un lac renversé
ni le ciel qui s'y reflète
mais simple condensation de fissures –
se met à calculer combien de soldats du passé
pourront tenir dans les nuages qui défilent :

et le printemps encore sous le choc de tant
de comptabilité hivernale
se mettra à son tour à additionner
puis à soustraire les divisions
de l'armée d'en face.

You in spring
when nature is still
UNDER THE SHOCK OF SNOWS
that fall no more
you when you re-count
cracks in the wall
or also when you re-count
cracks in your skin
or when you enumerate like a rosary
of stars torn from the prayer of the universe
the wrinkles in the earth's crust
or the crows' feet
that close your eyes:

when you repeat all that
the mountain
– the one that's no longer an overturned lake
nor the sky reflected in it
but pure condensation of fissures –
starts calculating how many soldiers of the past
the passing clouds can hold:

and spring still under the shock of so much
of winter's accountancy
starts in turn to add up
and then subtract the divisions
of the facing army.

Il a plu toute la journée
et ce soir quand les nuages
seront secs et tragiques
je rencontrerai
MON BUVEUR DE MÉMOIRE :

qui dit que la sécheresse lui doit beaucoup :

les pêcheurs d'eau douce
au moment de jeter leurs filets
aux mailles fines ne se fient pas :

ils regardent souvent
vers le ciel tant leurs rivières
leur semblent oublieuses :

il croient même que le souvenir
quand il s'évapore
s'en va dans les nuages
qui par hasard passent par là :

mais peut-on encore appeler nuage
un nuage engrossé de souvenirs :

et en voyant les pêcheurs lancer leurs filets
que peut bien penser une ville
quand dans son ciel défilent
comme un escadron d'avions ennemis
tous les monuments qu'elle n'y a pas érigés :

l'évaporation des souvenirs croit-on
serait un mouvement scientifiquement
tragique :

les souvenirs imiteraient la pluie
et ne retomberaient jamais à l'endroit
d'où ils auraient commencé leur ascension :

It rained all day
and this evening when the clouds
become dry and tragic
I'll meet
MY MEMORY-DRINKER:

who says that dryness owes him much:

the freshwater fishermen
in the moment of casting their nets
don't trust the fine mesh:

they look often
to the sky their rivers
seem so forgetful to them:

they even believe that memory
when it evaporates
moves into the clouds
passing there by chance:

but can one still call cloud
a cloud swollen with memories:

and seeing the fishermen cast their nets
what can a town be thinking
when in its sky like a squadron of enemy planes
all the monuments flash by
that it hasn't erected there:

the evaporation of memories
it is believed could be a scientifically
tragic movement:

the memories would imitate the rain
never falling in the place
from which they would have started their ascent:

ce serait le vent qui les pousserait:

mais peut-on encore appeler vent un vent
qui pousse les souvenirs :

et n'est-ce pas parce que le vent
n'est plus le vent
qu'ils lancent leurs filets
vers les nuages
qui ne sont plus les nuages
les pêcheurs alors que sous leurs barques
qui ne sont plus des barques
les avaleurs de mémoire
savourent leur festin :

et n'est-ce pas parce que je crois moins
aux nuages qu'à ce qui pourrait
monter là-haut
que ce soir
qui n'est plus un soir
j'ai rendez-vous avec mon mangeur de mémoire.

it'll be the wind that pushes them:

but can one still call wind a wind
that pushes memories:

and isn't it because the wind
is no longer the wind
that they throw their nets
towards the clouds that are no longer clouds
the fishermen
while under their boats
which are no longer boats
the memory-swallowers
savour their feast:

and isn't it because I think less
about clouds than what
could climb up there
that this evening
which is no longer an evening
I meet with my memory-eater.

Parmi les fatigues qui restent
laquelle garderais-tu
si l'arbre venait à disparaître :

si du tronc comme d'une ignorance de plus
ou de la brume tout autour se détachait
LA FIÈVRE DES CHOSES :

si chaque racine avait sa fatigue
et son tronc
qu'en garderais-tu :

et si à chaque racine était fixée une étiquette :

et si l'étiquette disait que ce qui disparaît
est ce qui reste quand tout autour
se détache des choses la fièvre
qu'en garderais-tu.

Among the remaining exhaustions
which one would you keep
if the tree came to disappear:

if breaking away from the trunk as if from
one more unknown or from surrounding mist was
THE FEVER OF THINGS:

if each root had its exhaustion
and its trunk
what would you keep:

if on each root was fixed a tag:

and if the tag said what is disappearing
and what remains when all around
the fever breaks away from things
what would you keep.

On ne va plus aujourd'hui
jusqu'au bord de la mastication
sans tourner plusieurs fois
LA POUSSIÈRE DANS LA BOUCHE :

quand ce qui est broyé sous les dents
fait demi-tour
et revient à son point de départ
tous les gardiens du dedans
comme ceux du dehors
avec leurs années sur leur dos
ou leurs pierres
ou leurs syllabes
poussent un cri de soulagement :

pas sûr que quelqu'un l'ait entendu :

pas sûr que le cri
s'il devait se reproduire
remette de l'ordre dans la bouche :

on ne va plus aujourd'hui
jusqu'au bord de la poussière
sans tourner plusieurs fois
la nostalgie dans la bouche.

Today you no longer reach
the edge of mastication
without several times turning over
THE DUST IN THE MOUTH:

when what's crushed between the teeth
goes halfway
and returns to its point of departure
all the guardians of inside
like those of outside
with their years on their backs
or their stones
or their syllables
heave a cry of relief:

not sure anyone heard it:

not sure that the cry
if it had to be reproduced
would restore order in the mouth:

today you no longer reach
the edge of dust
without several times turning over
nostalgia in the mouth.

Ce qui me précède comme emmêlé
dans un commencement étourdi
s'est infiltré
DANS LA FISSURE
apparue sur le flanc arrondi des souvenirs :

rien n'en revient
mais tout toujours tend
à s'en approcher
de là provient ce trouble
qui souvent accompagne le tremblement
du temps :

la volée d'oiseaux
qui obscurcit le plafond de la cuisine
n'est alors rien d'autre que le miroir
d'une crevasse fugace et noire
que l'oubli a laissée
par étourdissement sur la table
comme si du commencement
venaient des mots plutôt que
les choses :

puis quelqu'un invente un alphabet plus solide
et de ce qui ainsi s'apprivoise
une bonne moitié sinon plus
est destinée à jouer à la lettre p
le rôle du passé :

or p est aussi le père :

mais seulement au mois d'août
quand m est la mort
et que ce qui la précède porte mon nom.

That which goes before me as if
entangled in a heedless beginning
has infiltrated
THE CRACK APPEARING
on the rounded side of memories:

nothing returns from it
but everything is always trying
to approach it
from here comes the disturbance
that often accompanies the
time quake:

the flight of birds
that obscures the kitchen ceiling
is nothing other than the mirror
of a fleeting black crevasse
that forgetfulness left
heedlessly on the table
as if from the beginning
came rather words
than things:

then someone invents a more solid alphabet
and from everything tamed in this way
a good half if not more
is destined at the letter p to play
the rôle of the past:

but p is also paternal:

yet only in August
when d is death
and what precedes it bears my name.

L'ange qui chez mon poète a fui le ciel
avait envie d'une ombre à lui tout seul :

l'ombre on le sait est souvent capricieuse :

n'est-ce pas avec elle
qu'on rebouche les trous
qui çà et là apparaissent
dans ce bateau qui déjà prend l'eau :

c'est
UN BATEAU D'HIER
avec des marins superstitieux
et des mâts très hauts
et des voiles toutes gonflées :

des voiles qui fuient le ciel
et quand elles croisent l'ange
qui s'en éloigne
lui aussi en quête d'ombre
elles repensent à l'histoire de l'adolescent
aux ailes de cire :

n'est-ce pas avec son ombre
qu'on a rebouché les trous
de ce qui tombe.

(à Nuno Judice)

The angel who fled the sky in my friend's poem
wanted a shadow of his own:

shadow as everyone knows is often capricious:

isn't it with shadow
that we stop up the holes
appearing here and there
in this boat that's already leaking:

it's
A BOAT OF YESTERDAY
with superstitious sailors
and very tall masts
and swollen sails:

sails that flee the sky
and when they meet the angel
who moves away from them
also in search of shadow
they think once more of the youth
with wings of wax:

isn't it with his shadow
that we stopped up the holes
of all that falls.

(for Nuno Judice)

Dans l'épicerie fine de là-bas
les acheteurs de cigarettes en vrac
et de pincées de sel
que redoutent-ils sinon
LE SIGNAL DU MARCHAND
qui non loin de là
ne vend qu'en gros
les avrils vulnérables :

la pluie de mai il l'emballe
comme un jadis qui se plie facilement
dans une guitare
et la pose au pied des maisons mortes :

du soleil de l'été
il sortira la clé du doute :

et aux cordes qu'il dessinera
avec ce qui reste de regret
avant les grandes fontes de l'hiver
il suspendra les derniers naguères
de l'automne :

personne ne se retourne
dans l'épicerie fine de là-bas
quand non loin de là
de sa voix imbibée de vent
et de souvenirs d'argile
le marchand ordonnera au coq
d'entonner à tue-tête
l'hymne de l'ombre qui passe
et passant comme passe le temps
ou la mort
ne vient jamais sans son grain de sel :

l'ombre est noire on le sait
et le sel qui passe est blanc
comme le temps

In the grocers' down there
the buyers of loose cigarettes
and pinches of salt
what are they dreading if not
THE SIGNAL OF THE MERCHANT
who not far way sells
only vulnerable Aprils
wholesale:

the May rain he wraps it up
like a once that folds easily
inside a guitar
and puts it at the feet of dead houses:

from the summer sun
he'll take the key of doubt:

and from the ropes he draws
with what's left of regret
before the great thaws of winter
he'll hang the last long-agos
of autumn:

no-one turns round
in the grocers' down there
when not far away
with his voice soaked in wind
and memories of clay
the merchant will order the cock
to chant at full blast
the hymn of the shadow that passes
and passing like time passes
or death
never comes without its grain of salt:

the shadow is black as everyone knows
and the passing salt is white
like time

et dans la fumée noire
des cigarettes blanches achetées en vrac
dans l'épicerie fine de là-bas
quelque chose monte s'agenouiller aux pieds
du marchand d'avrils vulnérables :

et quand il pleut
à n'importe lequel de ces avrils-là
c'est le sel qui descend :

et ne dit-on pas
que le sel empêche de renaître.

(à Roberto Carosone)

and in the black smoke
of white cigarettes bought loose
in the grocers' down there
something goes up to kneel at the feet
of the merchant of vulnerable Aprils:

and when it rains
in any one of these Aprils
it's salt that comes down:

and don't they say
that salt prevents rebirth.

(for Roberto Carosone)

Dans l'œil de l'oiseau d'automne
avant qu'il ne parte
le jour paraît long :

long paraît aussi mais cela
nous ne le savons plus
le souffle qui tout autour
éteint et rallume les bougies :

nous creusons des métropolitains
dans leur cire
et aboutissons à des nuages
dont les contours perdent leur couleur
quand
TANT DE LUMIÈRE
y pénètre :

tout va vers l'absence
et à mesure que s'approche la clarté
le maintenant de ce qui reste
ressemble à l'oiseau d'automne
prêt à s'envoler :

nous le regardons
perché sur le vieux poteau noir
qui en a vu d'autres
et aimons nous dire
qu'entre celui qui en automne part
et l'autre qui au printemps reviendra s'y poser
il n'y a plus aucune ressemblance :

non que le voyage éteigne en eux
les longues bougies de l'oubli :

non que des longues bougies de l'oubli
comme d'un vieux poteau noir
dépende ce que l'automne a caché
dans l'œil de l'oiseau du printemps
avant qu'il ne parte.

In the eye of autumn's bird
before it leaves
the day seems long:

and it seems long too
though we no longer know this
the breath that all around
snuffs out and relights the candles:

we dig metro tunnels
in their wax
and end up at clouds
that lose their colours at the edges
when
SO MUCH LIGHT
gets in:

everything moves towards absence
and as clarity approaches
the now of what remains
looks like autumn's bird
ready to fly away:

we watch it
perched on the old black post
that has seen it all before
and like to say to ourselves
that between the one leaving in autumn
and the one that will land there in spring
there's no longer any resemblance:

not that the journey snuffs out in them
the long candles of forgetting:

not that on the long candles of forgetting
as if on an old black post
there hangs what autumn has hidden
in the eye of spring's bird
before it leaves.

L'après-midi claquant
comme claquait jadis la pétale du coquelicot
ou le fouet au cirque
ou au premier cinéma la stridence
d'une sonnerie de téléphone
en une nuit de lune absente
n'est pas à l'origine
ce fleuve qui monte et nous emplit :

qu'importe qu'un barrage se soit fissuré
en amont des choses
et de leurs rêves :

qu'importe qu'en aval
dans les champs ou sous les chapiteaux
le décompte ait déjà commencé :

un inondeur d'après-midis
a commencé son travail
et le nageur du dedans
comme un poisson pilote
sauve ce qui peut être sauvé :

il escorte les anecdotes qui restent
jusqu'à la lisière du souvenir :

ce sont des chiens sans maîtres dressant
HORS DE L'EAU
leurs secrets
à la moindre menace :

ce sont des après-midis de pluie de novembre :

devant les tombes ne se noie
que qui ne s'accroche pas à son parapluie :

lui aussi s'emplit de mort
à mesure que se noue le pacte avec le fleuve :

The afternoon cracking
like the poppy petal once cracked
or the circus whip
or first time at the cinema the harshness
of a telephone ringing
in a night of absent moon
is not originally
this river that rises and fills us:

what matter that a dam is split
upstream in things
and their dreams:

what matter that downstream
in the fields or in the marquees
the countdown has already started:

a flooder of afternoons
has set to work
and the swimmer of inside
like a pilot fish
saves what can be saved:

he leads the remaining anecdotes
up to the edge of remembering:

these are dogs without masters raising
their secrets
OUT OF THE WATER
at the slightest threat:

these are afternoons of November rain:

in front of the tombs the only one to drown
will be he who does not hang from his umbrella:

he also fills with death
as the pact with the river is sealed:

lui aussi se liquéfie
pour être plus souple
quand il reviendra :

est-ce pour cela qu'il sursaute
chaque fois que claque le fouet.

he also liquefies
to be more supple
when he returns:

is that why he jumps
each time the whip cracks.

C'est un désert parfois sans sablier :

un essaim de traces
pesant sur les sources épuisées :

il y a de la multiplication dans l'air
quand au-dessus des têtes passent
À BASSE ALTITUDE
les jardins volants :

tout y est double :

ce qu'on y plante et n'arrose jamais
ce qu'on y récolte sans le toucher
ce qu'on y enfouit sans le cacher :

tout y est double :

comme cette double épaisseur
qui soudain se glisse entre la vie
et ma mort.

It's a desert sometimes with no sandglass:

a swarm of traces
weighing on exhausted sources:

there's multiplication in the air
when overhead
the flying gardens pass
AT LOW ALTITUDE:

everything there is double:

what is planted there and never watered
what is gathered there without being touched
what is buried there without being hidden:

everything there is double:

like this double thickness
that slips suddenly between life
and my death.

Tout le silence est-il pour moi
comme l'est sur la paroi nord
de ce qui en moi parle
le vent ou ce qui s'en échapperait
ou parlerait
si parlait le soleil avant de se coucher :

le nord de la voix est rougissant :

et celui du vent
n'oublie pas de répandre
sa chevelure dormante
AU-DESSUS DES ARBRES :

et celui du couchant
ne connaît pas la solitude :

voilà qu'il soupèse son souffle
le triple nord du silence :

viens dit-il sur un ton aérien
viens poser sur le plateau bavard de la balance
un peu d'invisibilité :

viens peser sur l'équilibre du parler.

All the silence is it for me
as is the wind on the north face
of what speaks in me
the wind or what would escape from it
or speak
if the sun were speaking before setting:

the north of the voice is reddening:

and that of the wind
doesn't forget to spread
its sleeping hair
ABOVE THE TREES:

and that of sunset
doesn't know solitude:

now it weighs up its breath
the triple north of silence:

come it says in an airy tone
come and place on the talkative side of the scales
a little of the invisible:

come and weigh in the balance of speaking.

Du deuxième fleuve
comme d'un souvenir perdu
on ressort sans bagages :

tout est mis
À LA CONSIGNE
au fond de l'eau :

sur l'autre rive destinée
à qui ne sait encore se défaire
de ses manteaux
on remplit des bouteilles
et apparaissent
sur la branche inondée d'un olivier
ou au robinet de la sécheresse
ou au bout de l'épine plantée
dans l'âme du fugitif
des fantômes potables
dénués de consolation :

celui qui les appelle
comme on encourage le prisonnier
à escalader le mur
n'allume pas la torche qu'il agite :

il fait sombre quand tout renaît :

le feu n'est plus du côté du voleur.

From the second river
as if from a lost memory
you leave again without your bags:

everything is put
IN THE LEFT LUGGAGE
deep under water:

on the far side reserved
for the one who doesn't yet know how to
shed his coats
bottles are refilled
and there appear
on an olive tree's drowned branch
or at the tap of dryness
or at the end of the thorn planted
in the fugitive's soul
drinkable ghosts
devoid of consolation:

the one who calls them
as if urging a prisoner
to scale the wall
doesn't light the torch he's waving:

it's dark when everything comes back to life:

fire is no longer on the side of the thief.

Tant de soif
DANS LE COMMERCE DES SECRETS
n'alimente ni les soldeurs
ni les acheteurs de jours qui finissent :

qu'importe que sur les étals du soir
la sueur coule de nouveau
et que les corps
comme ceux d'un jour
jettent l'éponge au lieu d'absorber
les gouttes qui perlent
sur les fronts des coureurs :

n'est-ce pas ainsi
que ce qui est destiné aux yeux
file comme une eau usée
vers ce qui reste d'impatience :

n'est-ce pas ainsi
que pleure ses vainqueurs
le veilleur à l'entrée de la course.

So much thirst
IN THE SECRETS TRADE
feeds neither the discount sellers
nor buyers of ending days:

what does it matter that on the stalls of evening
sweat runs again
and that bodies
like those that last a day
throw in the towel instead of absorbing
the drops that pearl
on the runners' foreheads:

isn't it the case
that what's reserved for the eyes
drains like waste water
towards what's left of impatience:

isn't it the case
that he mourns his victors
the guardian at the entrance of the race.

Rappelle-toi que ce qu'à l'aube
tu as cru prendre pour de la poussière
sur la lune vieillissante
aurait pu être la dernière ombre de
LA FUITE DE LA NUIT
si en revenant de si loin sur la porte
claquée à toute vitesse
elle n'avait pas oublié de retirer
la clé de la serrure :

pourquoi en avoir honte
maintenant que l'heure approche
d'en revenir à la terre :

que celui qui contrairement à elle
n'a jamais fui
lance la première clé :

qu'il se souvienne en la lançant
que de la lune
ce que l'on pourrait prendre pour de la poussière
n'est souvent que l'ombre précoce
d'une porte claquée
qui quand de clés on parle
ou de serrures
sait que la lune en vieillissant le démentira :

elle n'en sera pas à un mensonge près
la lune quand la nuit reviendra :

elle n'en sera pas à une ombre près
la poussière :

rappelle-toi que ce que tu croiras prendre
pour de la poussière
sur la lune vieillissante
ne sera peut-être
que cette pincée de terre qui te manquera
quand la nuit reviendra.

Remember that what at dawn
you took for dust
on the ageing moon
could have been the last shadow of
NIGHT'S ESCAPE
if in returning from so far
to the door slammed in haste
it had not forgotten to take
the key from the lock:

why be ashamed of it
now that the hour approaches
for coming back to earth:

he who unlike night
has never escaped
should throw the first key:

he should remember in throwing it
that what from the moon
could be taken for dust
is often no more than the precocious shadow
of a slammed door
which when one speaks of keys
or of locks
knows that the moon as it ages will deny it:

one lie more won't matter
for the moon when night returns:

one shadow more won't matter
for the dust:

remember that what you'll take
for dust
on the ageing moon
will only be perhaps
this pinch of earth you'll miss
when night returns.

Et si chaque jour nous oubliions un mot :

ou le jetions à la poubelle
AVANT D'OUBLIER
le mot poubelle :

et toi tu oublierais quoi
pour commencer :

dis-moi tu commencerais par quel bout
toi à effacer l'univers.

And if every day we were to forget one word:

or throw it in the dustbin
BEFORE FORGETTING
the word dustbin:

what would you forget
to begin with:

tell me at which end you would begin
to erase the universe.

De :

Quatorze petits jeux de l'oubli et de la mémoire

J'ouvre le dictionnaire et parmi
LES COUPLES TRAGIQUES
que je passe en revue celui formé par l'oubli
et la mémoire restent étonnamment à l'écart :

l'obscurité et la lumière jouent à cache-cache
le jour et la nuit s'évitent de justesse mais
l'oubli et la mémoire se tiennent à l'écart
comme deux voyeurs cachés derrière le rideau :

on pourrait leur inventer une légende
qui veut qu'ils feignent tous deux
d'être nés aveugles :

tous les couples tragiques ont intérêt
à tricher avec le regard :

l'oubli et la mémoire trichent avec le regard :

quand l'un se retourne et que l'autre ne disparaît
pas ou quand c'est l'autre qui se retourne
tandis que l'un n'est pas changé en statue de sel
et que tous deux en profitent pour revenir
indemnes de là-bas l'hypothèse est simple :

ils feignent tous deux d'être nés aveugles :

ils trichent avec le regard l'oubli et la mémoire :

ils se trouvent derrière la fenêtre et écartent
légèrement le rideau et en bas dans la rue
ou plus loin sur le fleuve ou plus loin encore
derrière la forêt la nuit et le jour jouent
à cache-cache et l'obscurité et la lumière
s'évitent de justesse.

From:

Fourteen Little Games of Forgetting and Memory

I open the dictionary and among
THE TRAGIC COUPLES I see again
the one formed by forgetting and memory
stays amazingly withdrawn:

darkness and light play hide and seek
day and night narrowly avoid each other but
forgetting and memory withdraw
like two voyeurs behind a curtain:

you could invent them a legend
where they both pretend to have been
born blind:

all tragic couples have an interest
in cheating eyes:

forgetting and memory cheat with their eyes:

when one looks round and the other doesn't disappear
or when it's the other who looks round while
the one isn't changed into a pillar of salt
and when both of them take advantage of this to return
unharmed from that place the hypothesis is simple:

they both pretend to have been born blind:

they cheat with their eyes forgetting and memory:

there they are behind the window and they lightly
draw the curtain and down in the street
or further away on the river or further still
behind the forest night and day
play hide and seek and darkness and light
narrowly avoid each other.

Parmi
LES MOUCHES
qui se posaient un peu partout dans la cuisine
de jadis sur les tranches de pain ou le bord
des assiettes ou le ciré de la nappe
il y en avait une au moins qui ne jouait
pas le jeu :

rien ne la distinguait des autres sinon qu'elle
était une tache noire qui refusait de choisir
entre l'oubli et la mémoire :

je me suis dit elle doit venir de tout près
cette tache d'un destin en tout cas
moins aquatique que l'oubli :

ma mère qui avait tout compris n'y était
pas étrangère :

l'éponge à la main elle tournait le dos à la table :

et entre la tache et la mouche
elle ne choisissait pas :

quand la dernière poignée de terre a recouvert
le cercueil de mon père manquaient
déjà aux nuages l'une ou l'autre goutte
de pluie :

cela aurait pu continuer si nous étions restés
sur place :

plus tard dans la cuisine celui qui aurait osé
compter les taches aurait facilement pu
faire le lien :

mais il y en avait une qui ne jouait pas le jeu :

Among
THE FLIES
that settle everywhere in the kitchen
of long ago on the slices of bread or the
edges of plates or the wax of the tablecloth
there was at least one that wouldn't
play the game:

it was no different from the others except in that
it was a black stain refusing to choose
between forgetting and memory:

I told myself it must come from close by
this stain in any case from a less watery destiny
than forgetting:

my mother who had understood everything had
something to do with it:

sponge in hand she turned her back to the table:

and between the stain and the fly
she would not choose:

when the last handful of earth had covered
the coffin of my father already from the clouds
one or two drops of rain
were missing:

this could have continued if we'd
stayed put:

later in the kitchen anyone who'd dared
to count the stains could easily have
made the link:

but there was one that wouldn't play the game:

et son destin était plutôt terrestre :

et ma mère tournait le dos à la table :

et entre l'éponge et la table
elle ne choisissait pas.

and its destiny was more terrestrial:

and my mother would turn her back to the table:

and between the sponge and the table
she would not choose.

From:

EN RÉALITÉ

IN REALITY

2008

De : En réalité : les mots

Elle se colore soudain CETTE TERRE quand
tu la prends dans ta main et la réduis en poussière
comme si tu étais le tamis et elle l'or de nos
derniers jours et moi le chercheur aux mains vides.

et alors qu'elle se rapproche d'elle-même : je veux
dire : en tombant la poussière devient simple
éternité prise entre les deux pôles de son existence
sa chute répond moins à la règle du constant retour
qu'aux contraintes d'une gravité qui quand ta main
devient poussiéreuse s'empare de la matière.

c'est de là qu'est née la tristesse cosmique.

j'en vois l'effet mais pas la cause.

la perte de couleur universelle n'a pour moi d'autre
explication que le geste grave de ta poignée qui
prise de panique colorerait le système entier si
derrière lui : je veux dire : derrière le geste et non le
système ne se cachait pas la source d'où tout vient
mais rien ne part.

From: In Reality: Words

It blushes suddenly THIS EARTH when
you take it in your hand and crush it to dust
as if you were the sieve and it was the gold of our
last days and I the searcher with empty hands.

and so the earth comes to itself: I
mean: in falling the dust becomes just
eternity held between the two poles of its being
its fall answers less to the law of constant return
than to the limits of a gravity that when your hand
becomes dusty seizes matter.

this is how the sadness of the cosmos is born.

I see in this the effect but not the cause.

the loss of universal colour has for me no other
explanation than the grave gesture of your handful
that would colour the whole system in a fit of panic if
behind it: I mean: behind the gesture and not
the system there wasn't hiding the source from which
everything comes but nothing leaves.

Quand le vent s'est reposé et que rien ne s'est plus plié
à ses ordres je n'ai pu m'empêcher de chuchoter dans
ton oreille des mots courbés ramassés à la hâte avant la tempête.

puis j'ai repensé aux MÉTÉOROLOGUES.

de nous ils ne savent que ce que l'humidité leur a appris.

c'est mieux ainsi.

avant la tempête : je veux dire : avant la grande échelle
du début le vent traînait à ma fenêtre les parfums les
plus osés.

tout en était imbibé comme si du jardin universel nos
fleurs préférées nous faisaient un signe désespéré avant
de se disperser.

puis rien ne s'est plus plié aux ordres du vent et le gros
chêne devant la maison s'est conformément à la fable
brisé en deux : je veux dire : deux est la moindre des
choses : je veux dire n'as-tu pas vu que ces deux
troncs là-bas sont les derniers travers de la grande échelle.

When the wind came to rest and nothing followed
its orders any more I couldn't help whispering in your ear
bowed words gathered hastily before the storm.

then I thought again of METEOROLOGISTS.

of us they know only what humidity taught them.

it's better so.

before the storm: I mean: before the great ladder
of the beginning the wind was trailing at my window
the most daring perfumes.

everything was drenched in them as if our
favourite flowers were making desperate signs to us
from the universal garden before their dispersal.

then nothing bowed to the wind's commands any more
and the great oak in front of the house broke in two
according to the fable: I mean: two is the least of
things: I mean didn't you see that those two
trunks over there were the last rungs of the great ladder.

Tu as de la poussière cosmique sur le visage comme si le MÉTÉORITE DU DÉBUT avait fait escale en toi.

cela met la sérénité des vastes espaces dans ta respiration et me fait repenser à la charrette tiré par des bœufs ou au cerceau dévalant la pente de mon enfance.

la rose noire était déjà cultivée : je veux dire : avant tout cela quelqu'un avait fait signe aux éléments de se travestir.

l'un d'eux qu'on nommait alors encore le feu s'est souvenu de sa vie antérieure.

une autre charrette encastrée dans les rails du premier chemin de fer lui avait été fatale : je veux dire : ceux dont je viens et vers qui je vais sont ciselés sur le marbre de la stèle du monument aux morts.

il y a de la poussière sur leurs noms : je veux dire : en ce siècle-là on ne se nourrissait pas encore de pain et d'oignon mais de pépites ancestrales que les cœurs amassaient.

You have cosmic dust on your face as if the METEORITE
OF THE BEGINNING had stopped over in you.

this gives your breathing the serenity of vast spaces
and makes me think once more of the cart drawn by oxen
or the hoop hurtling down the slope of my
childhood.

the black rose was already cultivated: I mean: before
all that someone had made a sign to the elements
to disguise themselves.

one of them still named fire remembered
its previous life.

another cart wedged in the tracks of the first
railway had been fatal to it: I mean: those from whom
I came and towards whom I go are chiselled
on the marble slab of the monument to the dead.

there's dust on their names: I mean:
in that century one wasn't yet fed on
bread and onion but on raw ancestral gold
gathered by hearts.

J'ai fait un tour au cimetière pour entendre ce que
les noms des tombes me diraient.

avec toi à mes côtés le passé était facilement déclinable.

non que de l'assemblage aléatoire de l'alphabet
gravé dans la pierre une généalogie particulière ait
vu le jour.

des noms parcourus aucun ne faisait allusion
à ma destinée : je veux dire : c'est étonnant pour un
cimetière de ne pas se soumettre au devoir de me
rappeler que mon sort n'est en rien plus enviable
que celui de tous ces GISANTS ANONYMES immortalisés
par l'écriture.

I took a walk round the cemetery to hear what the names
on the graves would tell me.

with you at my side the past was easily declinable.

not that carved in the stone any particular genealogy
came to light from the chance
assemblage of the alphabet

none of the names I skimmed through made allusion
to my destiny: I mean: it's surprising for a cemetery
not to put itself to the task of reminding me that my fate
is no more enviable than that of all these
ANONYMOUS RECLINING FIGURES immortalised
by writing.

Un beau jour de cinquante comme tous ceux de MA GÉNÉRATION je suis tombé dans la parenthèse.

ceux qui avant tuaient industriellement étaient encore là : je veux dire : il y a eu un moment dans ma vie où côtoyé par des tueurs aînés j'ai continué à croire à l'innocence génétique.

puis on s'est mis à marcher sur la lune sans que cela modifie les axes élémentaires du système : je veux dire : personne n'a vu que ces petits pas là ne faisaient pas l'éloge de l'ombre mais sortaient comme d'une fumée familière.

quelqu'un s'est alors mis à recompter les étoiles et parvenu à la tienne plus brillante que jamais il a dit ce qu'on dit toujours en pareille situation : je veux dire : si après les charniers la nostalgie est encore possible ce n'est pas une parenthèse lunaire qui arrêtera la poésie : je veux dire : ne faudrait-il pas maintenant qu'un mur s'écroule.

One fine day of nineteen fifty like all those of MY
GENERATION I fell into parenthesis.

those who'd been killing industrially were still
at large: I mean: there was a moment in my life
where surrounded by older killers I continued
to believe in genetic innocence.

then they started walking on the moon without this
altering the elementary axes of the system: I
mean: no-one saw that those small steps
came not in praise of shadow but emerged
as if from familiar smoke.

someone then started re-counting the stars and
coming to yours brighter than ever he said
what everyone says in such situations: I
mean: if nostalgia is still possible after
the killing fields then no lunar parenthesis
is going to stop poetry: I mean: wouldn't
a wall now have to collapse.

Dans le couchant qui rougit ta chevelure les SERPENTS
DE L'HORIZON s'emmêlent les peaux : je veux dire : te
voilà serpentant dans l'air incandescent et rien de ce
qui fait le jour et la nuit ne te dissipe.

c'est ainsi que je te rêve et te rêve à nouveau jusqu'à
ce qu'aux éléments de base s'ajoute le travail
tranquille et secret de ma bibliothèque intime.

ce n'est pas facile à faire.

entre les blocs solides et liquides il n'y a guère de
concurrence : je veux dire : être l'un ou l'autre n'est
pas un choix.

mais quand ce qui est corps se déroule dans l'âme
en une lente soirée de fin d'été et qu'une main
repeint à l'intérieur ce que l'extérieur lui soustrait
c'est comme si de la terre à l'eau et plus loin encore
les porte-paroles du dedans sculptaient statue après
statue dans le creux des nuages : je veux dire :
là-bas entre chair et os notre amour ressemble
moins aux serpents qu'à l'incandescence rituelle
qui fait et défait l'horizon.

In the sunset that reddens your hair the SNAKES OF
THE HORIZON tangle in each other's skins: I mean:
there you are snaking in the incandescent air and nothing
of what makes day and night can dissipate you.

it's thus that I dream of you and dream of you again
up to where the base elements join the quiet
and secret work of my private library.

it's not easy to do.

between solid blocks and liquid there's almost no
competition: I mean: to be one or the other
is not a choice.

but when that which is body unfolds in the soul in a slow
evening at the end of summer and when just one hand
repaints inside with what outside took away from it
it's as if from the earth to the water and further again
the speakers of the inside were sculpting statue after
statue in the hollow of clouds: I mean:
there between flesh and bone our love less resembles
snakes than the ritual incandescence
that makes and unmakes the horizon.

Je ne me suis jamais posé la QUESTION DU RETOUR : je
veux dire : que l'on parte ou qu'on revienne est
dans la logique des choses : je veux dire : il ne suffit
pas que le voyage soit définitif pour qu'il cesse
d'être voyage.

quand je m'avançais vers toi ne comptait que la
distance parcourue.

elle était toujours constante comme si au fur et à
mesure que je marchais le sol sous mes pas et celui
sous les tiens se déplaçaient également : je veux
dire : ce qui voyageait en nous était ce lopin de terre
dont nous étions les extrémités immobiles.

I never asked myself the QUESTION OF RETURN: I
mean: that we leave or return is
in the logic of things: I mean: it's not
enough that the journey should be final for it to stop
being a journey.

when I was moving towards you nothing counted
but the distance travelled.

it was always constant as if while I
walked along the ground under my feet
and under yours moved equally: I
mean: what travelled in us was this clod of earth
of which we were the motionless extremities.

Quand dans l'embrasure d'une porte que je
voudrais extérieure apparaîtra et disparaîtra ta
silhouette je recompterai jusqu'à HUIT.

il y en a qui s'arrêtent à sept ou a trois d'autres vont
jusqu'à douze.

que chacun soit le comptable de sa propre mythologie.

mon huit à moi c'est deux fois quatre : je veux
dire : quand les quatre branches du bois droit
du cerf se sont plantées entre toi et moi et que les
quatre du bois gauche ont catapulté la bête dans
l'air leur somme n'était pas un calcul prémédité.

je suis sûr qu'il n'y avait pas huit cartouches dans
les fusils des chasseurs à la sortie de la
ville puisque ce n'était pas encore au tour de
l'animal du dedans de mourir cette nuit-là : je veux
dire : des huit possibilités du mourir plantées cette
nuit-là entre toi et moi aucune ne ressemblait
autant à la nôtre.

When in the crack of a door that I'd
like to be external your silhouette appears and disappears
I will count again up to EIGHT.   .

there are those who stop at seven or at three others who
go up to twelve.

everyone should be the accountant of his own mythology.

my own eight is two times four: I
mean: when the four branches of the stag's right antler
dug themselves in between you and me and the
four on the left catapulted the beast in
the air their total was not a premeditated sum.

I'm sure there were not eight cartridges in
the guns of the hunters at the edge of
town since it wasn't yet the turn of
the inner animal to die that night: I
mean: of the eight possible dyings planted that
night between you and me not one in the least
resembled our own.

From:

LE TRAVAIL DU POUMON

THE WORK OF THE LUNG

2007

Le nageur de l'ombre

I

PUISQUE JE VOIS AU PIED DU JAMAIS
le nuage à la nuit dormant.

Puisque j'entends dans dos de chemin trois
cloches et leurs pas vers le mourir.

Puisque je sens que de cet horizon-là
ou d'un autre un peu plus loin tombe en moi
l'oiseau maigre comme descend de très haut un
voyageur humide ou que coule de lui
la corde de mi-chemin.

Puisque son paquet est quelquefois
vieux cerf de mort ou alphabet
d'humide revenir. Puisque je fouille

dans les mots humides ou dans le jamais
de l'eau.

Puisque je fouille aussi dans une question qui fait
nuit – serait-ce toi respirant dans le nuage serait-ce
ton nom que j'entends dans le dos du jamais.

The Shadow Swimmer

I

SINCE I SEE AT THE FOOT OF NEVER
the sleeping cloud of night.

Since I hear behind the path's back three
bells and their steps towards dying.

Since I sense that from this horizon
or from another further one a meagre bird
falls inside me as from on high a
humid traveller descends or since running from it
is the rope of mid-way.

Since his burden is sometimes
old stag of death or alphabet
of humid returning. Since I search

inside the humid words or in the never
of water.

Since I search too inside a question that brings
night – would it be you breathing in the cloud would it be
your name that I hear at the back of never.

II

PUISQUE CHAQUE JOUR EST LETTRE BLANCHE
ou grammaire secrète battant poumon de pluie
ou résonnant du creux du matin ou se déplaçant
à la vitesse de l'ombre.

Puisque dans la liquéfaction des matins dort un cerf
un peu plus sombre ou que ton pull-over
est également un peu plus sombre que
jour sans remords ou rêve

sans rive. Puisque tout penche un peu vers l'eau.

Puisque pencher vers l'eau est programme profond
fenêtre donnant vers l'enfance.

Puisque quand je vois tant d'eau je pense à
sud précoce ou à mort de mon père
ou à bouche
fermée d'arbre provisoire.

Puisqu'il y a

herbe noire dans cette pensée-là
ou fruit obscur.

Puisque obscurité est olive calcinée
ou revers de main morte
ou départ vers l'arbre pauvre.

Puisque je mets mon visage dans l'épaisse somnolence
d'eau qui finit.

Puisque sans attendre l'extinction du feu.

Puisque je nage et nageant recolle les morceaux
du nageur de l'ombre.

II

SINCE EACH DAY IS WHITE LETTER
or secret grammar flagging lung of rain
or resounding from the hollow of the morning or moving
at the speed of shadow.

Since sleeping in the mornings' liquefaction is a stag
a little darker or since your pullover
is also a little darker than
day without remorse or borderless

dream. Since everything leans a little to water.

Since leaning to water is a deep plan
window opening on childhood.

Since when I see so much water I think of
precocious south or of death of my father
or of closed
mouth of provisional tree.

Since there is

black grass in that thought
or dark fruit.

Since darkness is calcified olive
or back of dead hand
or setting off towards the pauper tree.

Since I put my face in the thick somnolence
of water coming to an end.

Since without expecting the fire to go out.

Since I swim and swimming stick back the pieces
of the shadow swimmer.

III

PUISQUE TENTATION DU RETOUR N'EST PAS
morceau de papier aux montagnes sorties
comme d'une philosophie ou d'un
cheval à deux mors.

Puisque tunnel avec sa poignée
de roses muettes
ce devenir sans cesse un autre afin

que ne défile à l'intérieur un extérieur
robuste du moins
au premier plan

sinon un opaque conférencier
regard certainement laiteux porté à travers
le fil du revenir.

III

SINCE TEMPTATION TO RETURN IS NOT
a piece of paper with mountains emerging
as if from a philosophy or from a
horse with two bits.

Since tunnel with its handful
of silent roses
this becoming endlessly another so

that inside it's not an exterior parading
robust at least
in the foreground

but an opaque speaker
his decidedly milky regard carried through
the thread of return.

IV

PUISQUE JE NE PENSE PAS À FLOU NI
à grappes de guirlandes.

Puisque la saison ne met pas de longues branches bleues
dans le passé.

Puisque longues et bleues ne sont pas non plus les ignorances
agents de police au carrefour des caresses et des coups
de bois.

Puisque je ne pense pas à cerf de retour
ni à molle ouate
ou à long couteau qui lentement
l'achève.

Puisque toutes ces bouches ce soir ne mangent pas leurs
mots.

Puisque ne pas mettre cerf dans un poème
c'est éviter de parler de mort. Puisque

cerf n'a pas quatre lettres comme mort
le r là où il faut un peu avant la fin.

Puisque cerf ne vient pas pour rouler tambour comme on
roule les rêves quand méditerranée n'est pas loin.

Puisque r ne met pas du sud dans mort.
puisqu'il n'en met pas non plus dans cerf
puisqu'il n'en met pas non plus dans nord.

Puisque mort et cerf et nord ne sont pas
les trois derniers morceaux du trop respirer.

IV

SINCE I'M NOT THINKING OF BLUR NOR
clusters of garlands.

Since the season isn't placing long blue branches
in the past.

Since neither are they long and blue the unknowns
policemen at the crossroads of caresses and
antler-strikes.

Since I think neither of stag of return
nor soft cotton wool
nor long knife slowly
finishing it off.

Since all these mouths tonight do not eat their words.

Since not to put *cerf* in a poem
is to avoid mentioning death. Since

cerf doesn't have four letters like *mort*
the r in the right place just before the end.

Since *cerf* doesn't come to roll the drum as dreams are
rolled when mediterranean is nearby.

Since r doesn't put any south into *mort*
since neither does it put it into *cerf*
since neither does it put it into *nord*.

Since *mort* and *cerf* and *nord* are not
the last three morsels of too much breathing.

V

PUISQUE SE POURSUIVENT DANS LE PUITS
du cerveau l'obscurité indécise et sa frontière nord.

Puisque mordu par l'olivier mon père
fait nuit dans sa baleine.

Puisque mort est plus humide que nuit.

Puisque de baleine dépend parapluie noir
ou dernière chemise blanche
ou lacets noirs des chaussures et mains
croisées juste au-dessus de la ceinture.

Puisque noir est pâleur
qui a oublié les horloges
du trop voir.

Puisque de ces horloges-là descend
le pendule d'absence.

Puisque tout cela pousse dans le jardin du jamais.

Puisque dans jardin du jamais pousse
sans doute aussi oubli divisé ou
sa frontière pâle.

Puisque quand s'entrouvre la porte
n'entre pas vivre mais jamais.

V

SINCE CHASING EACH OTHER IN THE WELLS
of the brain are indecisive darkness and its northern frontier.

Since my father bitten by the olive tree
makes night in his whale.

Since death is more humid than night.

Since what hangs on whalebone is
black umbrella or last white shirt
or black laces for shoes and hands
crossed just above the belt.

Since black is paleness
that has forgotten the
clocks of too much seeing.

Since from these clocks descends
the pendulum of absence.

Since all this grows in the garden of never.

Since in garden of never
divided forgetting doubtless also grows
or its pale frontier.

Since when the door opens slightly
it's not living that enters but never.

VI

PUISQUE GRANDIES PAR LA NUIT LES FEUILLES
remontent vers l'olivier.

Puisque signal n'est pas encore donné.

Puisqu'il y a sang et son contraire dans trace
de nuit et que monte d'absence
une colonne de noir.

Puisqu'un train patient orchestre les
rails du poumon.

Puisque quand ses roues sautent sur les cerfs
de la peur un œil s'ouvre à l'angle triste
de chaque ombre.

Puisque comme si un œil s'ouvrait
à angle triste de chaque ombre.

VI

SINCE SWOLLEN BY NIGHT THE LEAVES
climb back to the olive tree.

Since signal is not yet given.

Since there is blood and its opposite in trace
of night and since rising from absence is
a column of black.

Since a patient train orchestrates the
tracks of the lung.

Since when its wheels jump at the stags
of fear one eye opens at the sad corner
of each shadow.

Since as if one eye was opening
at the sad corner of each shadow.

VII

PUISQUE SORTIR DEUX MOUCHOIRS DE LA
poche est un mouvement diagonal.

Puisque sur la ligne de partage entre deux mouchoirs
se traîne un réveil humide.

Puisque triste est un mot humide
avec deux bords comme chaque solitude.

Puisque d'humidité vient et ne s'en va pas
brûlure solitaire est-ce doute de chaleur
devant tant d'ardence ou angoisse de chemin
rare quand arrivent les huit dernières
vérités de nuit d'été.

Puisque quand brûle le chemin
un cerf calciné ramasse les cailloux
de la respiration.

VII

SINCE PULLING TWO HANDKERCHIEFS FROM A
pocket is a diagonal movement.

Since on the dividing line between two handkerchiefs
a humid awakening drags itself along.

Since sad is a humid word
with two edges like every solitude.

Since humidity comes and doesn't leave
lonely burning is it wariness of heat
before such blaze or anxiety of rare
path when the last eight truths
of a summer's night arrive.

Since when the path burns
a calcinated stag picks up the small stones
of breathing.

VIII

PUISQUE LES CAILLOUX QU'ON RAMASSE
effacent le chemin non la main
qui palpe les mots furieux.

Puisque de mot à mort erre une consonne furieuse.

Puisque comment se fait-il que consonne
furieuse erre entre mot et mort.

Puisque quand mon père meurt
toutes les consonnes sont furieuses.

Puisque tant de fureur
lancée contre le mur du pourquoi
ne blesse ni le mur ni pourquoi.

VIII

SINCE THE SMALL STONES YOU GATHER
erase the path not the hand
that fingers the furious words.

Since from *mot* to *mort* errs a furious consonant.

Since how is it that a furious consonant
errs between *mot* and *mort*.

Since when my father dies
all the consonants are furious.

Since so much fury
thrown against the wall of why
injures neither the wall nor why.

IX

PUISQU'ELLE EST CONTENTE DE SON PIED
l'étrange montagne.

Puisqu'elle ne trahit pas le village ni
les pieds qui d'un côté écrasent le raisin
de la veille.

Puisque dans hier du mourir ne bouge pas
l'écrasement traversé par un cerf.

Puisque d'animal sacrifié ne sort pas
à condition d'être
de ce côté-ci du sacrifice
montagne.

Puisque de l'autre côté de sacrifice
on aplatit également les cœurs.

Puisque les deux sangs de sacrifice
se rejoignent dans
l'épicentre d'animal travesti.

Puisque figuier se transforme en pommier.

Puisque tant de trahison bout dans la marmite
du demain.

Puisque dans celle du hier ne bout que voyage
sans aujourd'hui.

IX

SINCE IT IS HAPPY WITH ITS FOOT
the strange mountain.

Since it betrays neither the village nor
the feet that on one side crush
grapes from the previous day.

Since inside dying's yesterday the crushing
crossed by a stag isn't moving.

Since mountain
does not come from sacrificed animal
as long as it's
this side of the sacrifice.

Since on the other side of sacrifice
they also flatten hearts.

Since the two bloods of sacrifice
meet in the epicentre
of disguised animal.

Since fig tree turns into apple tree.

Since so much treason is boiling in
tomorrow's pot.

Since in yesterday's nothing boils but journey
without today.

X

PUISQUE PULL-OVER NE CESSE DE BLEUIR.

Puisque dans bleu brille la cloche
de ce qui ne vient pas quand les mots
font le travail du poumon.

Puisque faire un tel travail pose un autobus bleu
sur les épaules de mon père.

Puisque dans ce voyage-là on n'a pas besoin
de lacets aux dernières chaussures.

puisqu'on y frappe aux carreaux de l'œil.

Puisque bleu est couleur voyageuse.

Puisque bleuir est galet qui tombe dans l'eau.
Puisque bleuir est épaule sud de mon père.
Puisque épaule nord touche corps inertes
ou terre rouge ou wagons à décrocher.

Puisque d'épaule à épaule les vivants
ne font que le travail du poumon.

X

SINCE PULLOVER DOESN'T CEASE TURNING BLUE.

Since in blue shines the bell
of what doesn't come when the words
do the work of the lung.

Since doing such work sets a blue bus
on my father's shoulders.

Since on that journey laces on the last shoes
aren't needed.

Since there you knock on the eye's window pane.

Since blue is a travelling colour.

Since turning blue is pebble falling into water.
Since turning blue is south shoulder of my father.
Since north shoulder touches inert bodies
or red earth or wagons to unhook.

Since shoulder to shoulder the living
do nothing but the work of the lung.

XI

PUISQUE DANS LA BANLIEUE DU RÊVER
erre une lumière ridée.

Puisque perte n'est pas le mouchoir sacré dont
on recouvre les visages.

Puisque quand soufflent les brises l'haleine
de l'horloger fige comme une méditerranée arrêtée
le paraître de mémoire.

Puisque mémoire est armoire

ou manteau ou feuille
d'horloger tombée.

Puisque rien ne bouge dans le souffler
ni poids de silence ni aiguilles de vent. Puisque

tu as vu la chemise baleinée tromper
le parapluie de la mort.

Puisque

le paysage qui en découle est tango
derrière un paravent de paupières mortes
sous-sol d'hôpital
ou orchestre du simple aimer.

Puisque être tango brise non
le cœur mais battre.

XI

SINCE IN THE SUBURBS OF DREAMING
errs a wrinkled light.

Since loss is not the sacred handkerchief with which
faces are covered.

Since when breezes blow the clockmaker's
breath like a stopped mediterranean fixes
memory's appearing.

Since memory is wardrobe

or coat or clockmaker's
fallen leaf.

Since nothing moves in the blowing
neither weight of silence nor wind's hour hands. Since

you saw the whaleboned shirt
cheat death's umbrella.

Since

the landscape that arises is tango
behind a screen of dead eyelids
hospital basement
or orchestra of simple loving.

Since to be tango breaks not
the heart but beating.

XII

PUISQUE DE BOUCHE SORT LE CARREAU
d'une voix d'œil brisée.

Puisque de bouche à bouche disparaissent
jours lâchés lampes intérieures paupières
du penser.

Puisqu'on déchire les retards dont on s'habille.

Puisqu'en prononçant retard se rétablit
l'équilibre du poumon même si se
penche de la bouche un départ aveugle
ou déguisé
en horloge involontaire.

Puisqu'en prononçant horloge il y a
liquéfaction des voix.

Puisqu'en prononçant horloge il y a
paupière de l'autre penser.

Puisque l'autre penser est une louche
de dedans quand il n'est pas pincée
de sel du dehors.

Puisque lire dans le sel est statue.

Puisque d'elle à bouche
se brisent voix et œil.

XII

SINCE OUT OF MOUTH COMES THE WINDOW
pane of eye's broken voice.

Since from mouth to mouth released
days interior lights thinking's eyelids
disappear.

Since you tear up the delays you're dressed in.

Since in pronouncing delay the balance
of the lung is re-established even if
a blind departure leans from the mouth
or disguised
as involuntary clock.

Since in pronouncing clock there is
liquefaction of voices.

Since in pronouncing clock there is
eyelid of the other thinking.

Since the other thinking is a ladle
of inside when it isn't pinch of
salt from outside.

Since reading in salt is statue.

Since from statue to mouth
voice and eye are breaking.

XIII

PUISQUE S'EST ARRÊTÉE LA LOCOMOTIVE
du penser malade.

Puisque le corps lourd du voyage s'enfonce
dans l'arrêt.

Puisque dans le jour qui se rhabille un long
partir refait ses comptes.

Puisqu'il fait long et lourd sur la table
des années comptées.

Puisque vers la source vont l'avoir vécu
et ses images qui grandissent encore.

Puisque appeler cela un peu de cœur
ou fond de mer ou mélange abandonné
de vieux silence
et de locomotive obscure.

Puisque table est désir inoccupé.

Puisque au penser pendent des fruits malades.

Puisque comment se fait-il qu'au penser
pendent des fruits malades.

XIII

SINCE THE LOCOMOTIVE
of sick thinking has stopped.

Since the heavy body of the journey sinks
in the stop.

Since in the day that dresses itself again
a long leaving remakes its accounts.

Since it is long and heavy on the table
of counted years.

Since they go to the source the having-lived and
its still-growing images.

Since to call this a piece of heart
or ocean floor or abandoned mixture
of old silence
and dark locomotive.

Since table is unoccupied desire.

Since sick fruit hangs on thinking.

Since how is it that sick fruit
hangs on thinking.

XIV

PUISQUE RIEN NE ME POUSSE HORS DU FEU.

Puisque devant la grotte du prononcer
flotte un drapeau mortel.

Puisque dans l'oiseau de ton sourire
tous les drapeaux sont mortels.

Puisque demain arriveront chiffres
et cendres et chiffons
de mots déprononcés.

XIV

SINCE NOTHING PUSHES ME OUT OF THE FIRE.

Since before the cave of pronouncing
flies a mortal flag.

Since in the bird of your smile
all flags are mortal.

Since tomorrow come ciphers
and ashes and rags
of depronounced words.

XV

PUISQUE CE VIOLENT OBSCUR EST BEAUCOUP
moins dur que les tenailles de la nuit.

Puisqu'il vaut moins que ton pare-brise dans l'éclat
de voix et plus
qu'une fin
de poitrine épargnée.

Puisque si moins de jardin chante à la périphérie
du sel et de ses cendres
et moins de couleur
et plus de volonté.

Puisque moins de jardin ne fait pas plus de volonté.

Puisque si chanter moins lourd ou
moins chaud ou plus dehors
ou moins nord
ou moins nord encore
ne signifie pas que la nuit s'apprête à
bleuir l'alphabet de ton pull-over.

Puisque dans le lit d'alphabet coule une rivière
plus étroite que le revenir de là où moins
et plus sont le charbon triste du désamour.

Puisqu'il y a moins de désert dans les cendres
d'alphabet et plus de mémoire.

Puisque personne ne parle de feu ni de canots
de sauvetage.

Puisque parler ne vaut pas grand-chose
par les souvenirs qui soufflent.

XV

SINCE THIS VIOLENT DARK IS FAR
less harsh than the pincers of night.

Since it's worth less than your windshield in the shattering
of voice and more
than an ending
of spared chest.

Since if less garden sings at the periphery
of salt and its ashes
and less colour
and more will.

Since less garden does not make more will.

Since if singing less heavy or
less hot or more outside
or less north
or still less north
does not mean the night is about to
turn your pullover's alphabet blue.

Since in the alphabet's bed runs a river
narrower than returning from where less and more
are the sad coal of unlove.

Since there is less desert in the alphabet's
ashes and more memory.

Since no-one speaks of fire nor of
lifeboats.

Since talking's not worth all that much
when memories blow by.

XVI

PUISQU'EN ANNÉE DE BEAU PARLER
on n'allume ni cierges ni repentirs.

Puisque la feuille ne renie pas l'arbre tombé.

Puisque le nuage ne renie pas le ciel du dedans.

Puisque qui lance le premier lierre
est le dernier proxénète de la lumière.

Puisque partir n'est qu'une métaphore du rester.

XVI

SINCE IN A YEAR OF BEAUTIFUL TALK
one lights neither candles nor regrets.

Since the leaf does not disown the fallen tree.

Since the cloud does not disown the inner sky.

Since he who throws the first ivy
is the last procurer of light.

Since leaving is only a metaphor for staying.

XVII

PUISQUE DANS LE CIMETIÈRE DE LA LUMIÈRE
on ne cueille que des olives noires.

Puisque si aucun mal n'est fait aux conférenciers du silence.

Puisque si on ne parle que par bouteilles interposées
ou mains qui de loin les repêchent
ou coups de rames pour mourir
ou cols de chemises à amidonner.

Puisque si de ton bras ne dépend aucune valise.

Puisque si la moitié du temps est écoulée.

Puisque si de l'horizon du parler descendent l'oubli
géant et les ailes qui l'empêchent d'oublier.

Puisque si cherchant dans descente on trouve
soleil sec ou linge étendu au pied
du revenir.

Puisque si cherchant dans revenir on trouve
soleil étendu au pied du linge sec.

Puisque tant de sécheresse.
Puisque tant de revenir.

XVII

SINCE IN THE CEMETERY OF LIGHT
we can gather only black olives.

Since if no harm could come to the lecturers of silence.

Since if we only speak by means of bottles
or hands that fish them out from far away
or strokes of oars for dying
or shirt collars for starching.

Since if no suitcase hangs on your arm.

Since if half of time has drained away.

Since if giant forgetfulness descends from the horizon of
speech with wings that hinder its forgetting.

Since if searching in descent we find
dry sun or washing spread at the foot
of returning.

Since if searching in returning we find
sun spread at the foot of dry washing.

Since so much dryness.
Since so much returning.

XVIII

PUISQUE DU SORTIR DE LA BOUCHE SE FREINE
le corps du lent répondre.

Puisqu'il fait minuit sur les deux plateaux
du parler. Puisque minuit est la face nord du parler.

Puisque parler est la côte tarie de l'origine.

Puisque quand je parle le tunnel du parler
devient plus long et plus noir.

Puisque ce qui parle en moi est accoudé à un mur.
Puisqu'il y a une fenêtre dans ce mur.

Puisqu'il y a une fenêtre entre ce qui parle en moi
et le moi qui parle.

Puisque du sortir du mur le corps
ressemble à une parole penchée.

XVIII

SINCE WHILE LEAVING THE MOUTH
the body of slow answering decelerates.

Since it's midnight on both sides of the scales
of speaking. Since midnight is the north face of speaking.

Since speaking is the origin's dried rib.

Since when I speak the tunnel of speaking
grows longer and darker.

Since what speaks in me leans against a wall.
Since there is a window in this wall.

Since there's a window between what speaks in me
and the I that speaks.

Since while leaving the wall the body
looks like a tilted word.

XIX

PUISQUE À LA PORTE EST SUSPENDUE
une clé de sourire.

Puisque d'elle s'effondre la grammaire du répondre.

Puisque s'effondre également
la grammaire du demander.

Puisque répondre et
demander sont lentes métaphores
de serrure sans centre

porte qui longuement finit

clé de lumière ensevelie.

XIX

SINCE AT THE DOOR HANGS
a key of smiling.

Since in this the grammar of answering collapses.

Since the grammar of asking
also collapses.

Since answering and
asking are slow metaphors for
lock without centre

door that lengthily finishes

key of buried light.

XX

PUISQUE FÊLURE ET BROUILLARD OUVRENT
la flamme du flou respirer.

Puisque respirer n'a pas d'ombre.

Puisque l'ombre est l'aînée de la flamme.

Puisque le feu de l'imprononçable donne
ses couleurs à la robe du simple aimer.

Puisqu'un petit souffler suffit pour
éteindre les bougies de l'imprononçable.

Puisque es-tu fêlure et brouillard

ou plutôt flamme du flou respirer.

XX

SINCE CRACK AND FOG OPEN
the flame of blurred breathing.

Since breathing has no shadow.

Since shadow is the flame's elder.

Since the fire of the unpronouncable gives
its colours to the dress of simple loving.

Since a small breath is enough to
blow out the candles of the unpronounceable.

Since are you crack and fog

or rather flame of blurred breathing.

XXI

PUISQUE LA PIERRE DU SILENCE EST LOURDE.

Puisqu'il y a fureur entre les paroles
ou lourde feuille de nuit ou train
de jour.

Puisque quand part le train ce n'est pas
train qui compte mais départ.

Puisqu'il y a ce jet d'eau dans musique
du départ que personne ne voit.

Puisque musique du départ est mouillée.

Puisque ce qui se déplace quand on part
ce n'est pas musique mais humidité.

XXI

SINCE THE STONE OF SILENCE IS HEAVY.

Since there was fury between the words
or heavy sheet of night or train
of day.

Since when the train leaves it's not
train that counts but leaving.

Since there's this jet of water in music
of leaving that nobody sees.

Since music of leaving is moist.

Since what moves when one leaves
it's not music but humidity.

Translator's Acknowledgements

Acknowledgements and thanks are due to Le Castor Astral, Éditions Phi, Red Fox Press and the *Kenyon Review*, where the original poems and some of the translations from this book have been previously published.

Thanks to Patrick McGuinness and Nicola Frith, whose insights were invaluable at certain stages of this project, and above all to Jean Portante for his patient and illuminating explanations in our many discussions of these poems.

The Author

Jean Portante was born in 1950 in Differdange, Luxembourg, and now lives in Paris. He has written novels, stories, plays, journalism and poetry. Translations of his work into numerous languages include, in English, *Point/Erasing*, by Anne Marie Glasheen (Daedalus, 2003). He is a translator of poetry into French from Spanish, Italian, English and German. His novels include *Mrs Haroy ou la mémoire de la baleine* (Éditions Phi, 1997), which has been widely translated, and he is also the author of the biography *Allen Ginsberg: L'autre Amérique* (Le Castor Astral, 1999).

Portante's collection of poems *L'étrange langue* (Éditions Le Taillis Pré, 2002) won the Prix Mallarmé in France in 2003, and the same year he was given the Grand Prix d'Automne de la Société des Gens de Lettres for his entire life's work in poetry. In 2005, Le Castor Astral published a selected poems, *La cendre des mots*, covering his work from 1989 to 2005. Since 2006 he has been a member of the Académie Mallarmé. In 2008 he co-founded the French poetry magazine *Inuits dans la jungle* with the poet Jacques Darras, while in Luxembourg he heads the literary magazine *Transkrit*. In 2011 he was awarded Luxembourg's Batty Weber National Prize, which is given every three years for a life's work. His latest books are *Conceptions* (Éditions Phi, 2012) and *Après le tremblement* (Éditions Le Castor Astral, 2013).

The Translator

Zoë Skoulding has published four collections of poetry, most recently *Remains of a Future City* (Seren, 2008), which was long-listed for Wales Book of the Year 2009, and *The Museum of Disappearing Sounds* (Seren, 2013). She is the editor of the international quarterly *Poetry Wales*, and Senior Lecturer in the School of English at Bangor University.